Cutting and Pasting

Written by Jennifer Dryden
Illustrations by Steve Mack

New York

New York

An Imprint of Sterling Publishing
387 Park Avenue South
New York, NY 10016

ISBN 978-1-4114-5807-9 (paperback)

Distributed in Canada by Sterling Publishing
c/o Canadian Manda Group, 165 Dufferin Street
Toronto, Ontario, Canada M6K 3H6
Distributed in the United Kingdom by GMC Distribution Services
Castle Place, 166 High Street, Lewes, East Sussex, England BN7 1XU
Distributed in Australia by Capricorn Link (Australia) Pty. Ltd.
P.O. Box 704, Windsor, NSW 2756, Australia

For information about custom editions, special sales, and premium and corporate purchases, please contact Sterling Special Sales at 800-805-5489 or specialsales@sterlingpublishing.com.

Manufactured in Canada
Lot #:
4 6 8 10 9 7 5 3
12/12

www.flashkids.com

Dear Parent,

Cutting and Pasting offers simple and complex activities that progress from cutting straight lines and zigzags to pasting different pieces together to create scenes. These fun exercises build essential fine motor skills and teach your child to follow simple directions. Tear each page out and encourage your child to begin cutting on either side, depending on whether he or she is left- or right-handed. As you work through this book together, offer guidance on difficult activities, but allow your preschooler to attempt challenges independently. When the workbook is complete, reward your child with the certificate on page 79. For free downloads and fun activity ideas, visit www.flashkids.com.

Have your child put his or her thumb into the small hole in the scissors and his or her pointer and middle finger in the larger hole. Then have your child hold the scissors straight and level with the paper, taking care not to point the scissors up or down. Ask your child to practice opening and closing the scissors while holding the paper steady. Remember: "Open, shut. Open, shut… cut, cut, cut!"

People walk along busy sidewalks.
Cut along the lines from (●) to (●).

People get around the city in taxis.
Cut along the lines from (●) to (●).

Some buildings are tall.
Cut out the building.

Some buildings are short.
Cut out the building.

Cut out the windows and door.
Paste them on the building.

Trains are one way to travel in the city.
Cut out the train cars.
Paste them together to make one long train.

Buses get people around the city, too.
Cut out the windows.
Paste them to the bus.

Houses are close together in the city.
Cut along the line from (●) to (●).

Help the children get to school in the city.
Cut along the line from (●) to (●).

Firefighters keep the city safe.
Help them get to the fire.
Cut along the line from (●) to (●).

Pizza is one yummy food you can find in the city. Cut out the slices.

Kites fly high in the city park!
Cut out the kites. Paste them to the strings.

City kids love to play at the playground.
Cut along the line from (●) to (●).

Workers hang signs in the city.
Cut out the sign.

Bridges stretch from one part of the city to another.
Cut along the line from (●) to (●).

Help Metro find his way through the park.
Cut along the line from (●) to (●).

EXIT

Metro needs a drink from the hose.
Cut along the line from (●) to (●).

The park has a colorful carousel.
Cut out the carousel.

This man sells bubbles at the fair.
Cut out the bubbles.

BUBBLES

The city is fun by day or night.

Cut out the sun and moon. Paste them in the sky.

Bicycles are a healthy way to get around.
Cut out the wheels.
Paste them on the bicycle.

Honk! Honk!
Cut out the tires.
Paste them on the taxi so it can go, go, go!

Metro sees a squirrel!
Cut out the acorns. Paste them on the tree.

Keeping the city clean is important.
Cut out the cans. Paste them in the bin.

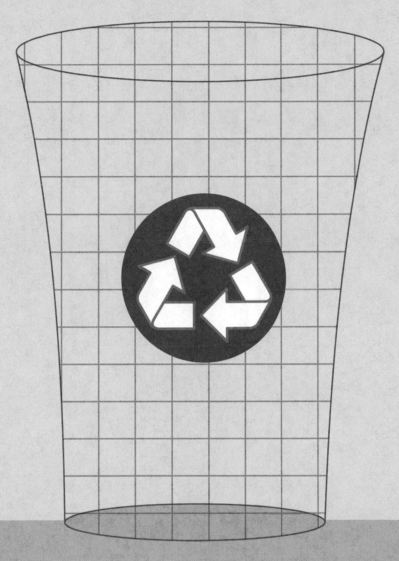

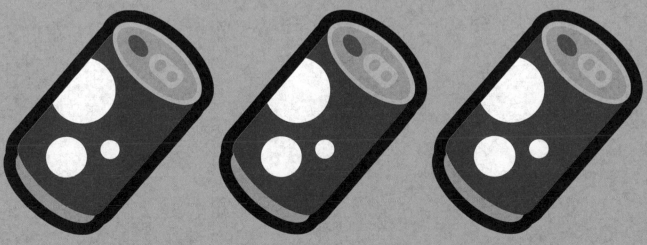

Buses, cars, and trucks travel through the city. Cut out the vehicles. Paste them to the road.

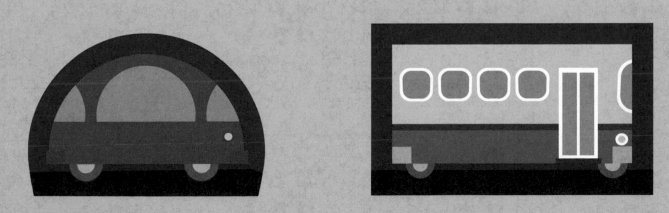

Make a wish!
Cut out the coins.
Paste them in the fountain.

A skyscraper is a tall building.
Cut out the parts of the building.
Paste them together.

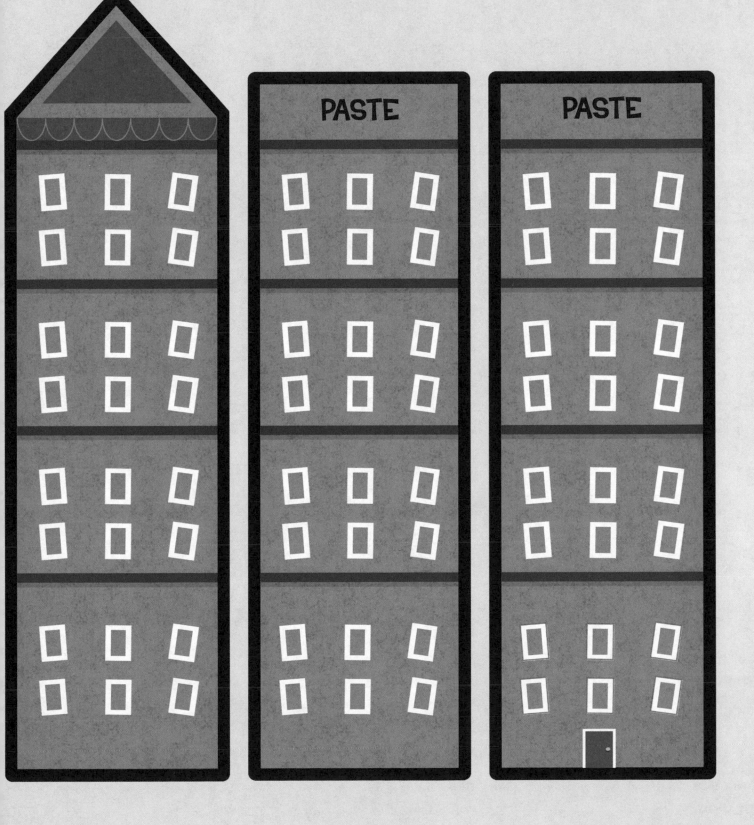

The clock tower tells the time.
Cut out the clock. Paste it on the building.

Sail away with Metro!
Cut out the sails. Paste them on the boats.

The city has many stores.
Cut along the black lines. Put the puzzle together.

Visitors come to the city on a cruise ship. Cut out the flags. Paste them on the ship.

What's up in the air?
Put the puzzle together to find out!

Toy stores are fun places!
Cut out the toys. Paste them in the window.

Toy Store

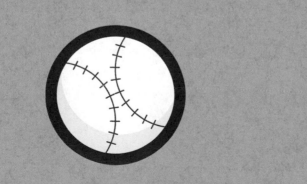

Ice skating takes practice.
Cut out the skaters. Paste them on the rink.

In the city, people can buy snacks from carts.
Cut out the umbrella. Paste it to the cart.

Metro wants to be your friend.
Cut him out and take him home!

Congratulations!

_____

has successfully completed
Cutting and Pasting.